Jeet Kune Do Unlimited

A Jeet Kune Do Concepts Guidebook

By Burton Richardson

Disclaimer

Although both Unique Publications and the author(s) of this martial arts book have taken great care to ensure the authenticity of the information and techniques contained herein, we are not responsible, in whole or in part, for any injury which may occur to the reader or readers by reading and/or following the instructions in this publication. We also do not guarantee that the techniques and illustrations described in this book will be safe and effective in a self-defense or training situation. It is understood that there exist a potential for injury when using or demonstrating the techniques herein described. It is essential that before following any of the activities, physical or otherwise, herein described, the reader or readers first should consult his or her physician for advice on whether practicing or using the techniques described in this publication could cause injury, physical or otherwise. Since the physical activities described herein could be too sophisticated in nature for the reader or readers, it is essential a physician be consulted. Also, federal, state or local laws may prohibit the use or possession of weapons described herein. A thorough examination must be made of the federal, state and local laws before the reader or readers attempts to use these weapons in a self-defense situation or otherwise. Neither Unique Publications nor the author(s) of this martial arts book guarantees the legality or the appropriateness of the techniques or weapons herein contained.

To contact Burton Richardson,

or for more information on Jeet Kune Do Unlimited Membership, Seminars, Phase Testing, or Certification, call or write to the international headquarters:

Burton Richardson
Jeet Kune Do Unlimited
934 Hermosa Ave. #5
Hermosa Beach, CA 90254

310-318-6866 Telephone
310-318-8535 Fax

or visit the Jeet Kune Do Unlimited website at www.jkdunlimited.com

ISBN: 0-86568-167-8
Library of Congress Catalog Number: 97-62167

UNIQUE PUBLICATIONS
4201 Vanowen Place, Burbank, CA 91505

Dedication

This book is dedicated to

My Mother who exemplifies the spirit of giving.

My Father who rewarded me for being honest and taught me how to work hard. He also taught me to listen to everyone, then use what works best for me.

My sifu, Dan Inosanto. Living proof of the power of the Jeet Kune Do Concept. His skill and generosity know no bounds.

June Castro. Thanks for everything.

Martial art students everywhere. TRAIN WELL AND ENJOY!

To everyone who has helped me along my path, including: Richard Bustillo, Paul de Thouars, Chai Sirisute, Herman Suwanda, Larry Hartsell, Paula Inosanto, Catherine Lopez, Steve Grody, Francis Fong, Chris Kent, Tim Tackett, Bert Poe, Bud Thompson, Don Familton, Mark Mikita, Eric Knauss, Mark Denny, Sam Tendencia, Leo Gaje, Leo Giron, Yorinaga Nakamura, The Machado Brothers, Egan Inoue, the Carlson Gracie group, Vitor Belfort, Wally Jay, Jon Tessier, Ralph Castro, Salem Assli, Paul Vunak, Cassimore Magda, Antonio Illustrisimo, Tony Diego, Christopher Ricketts, Edgar Sulite, Bert Labaniego, Hal Faulkner, Garth Redwood, Daniel Duby, Mike Mentzer, Dennis Alexio, Joseph Hallabay, Bob Bragg, Anthony Robbins. Special thanks goes to Curtis Wong, the staff at Unique Publications, and everyone else I should have mentioned.

Special thanks to those who assisted me in the photos. Jesse Anderson, Ralph Bustamante, June Castro, Lester Griffin, Wally Kronberger, Ray Rosales and Richard Rycraw.

Table of Contents

Introduction

Chapter 1
The Philosophy of the Jeet Kune Do Concept

Chapter 2
The Art of the Jeet Kune Do Concept

Chapter 3
Examples of the Jeet Kune Do Concept

WHY I WROTE THIS BOOK

First and foremost, I wrote this book so that I could share some of the insights I have earned through years of training. I share this because I hope that everyone who takes up the study of Martial Arts will have as much enjoyment and personal growth as I have. Hopefully, this book will make the journey a little easier.

I also hope to encourage students and teachers of the arts to be as complete as possible in their approach. This means studying in all ranges and from all cultures. It means getting real experience in each range of fighting, not just learning techniques and drills. It also means doing your best to become a living example of the moral and philosophical codes that have been passed down. Being kind and forgiving to yourself and others takes as much training as being able to defend yourself!

Have fun, enjoy the process, and may you have the wisdom and strength to make every experience a catalyst for greater understanding and personal growth.

Sincerely,

Burton Richardson

CHAPTER 1
The Philosophy of the Jeet Kune Do Concept

The Jeet Kune Do Concept is more than just punching and kicking. It is a way of developing yourself in every area of your life. Understanding the philosophies and tactics of the art will improve you as a person and propel you toward your goals.

The Jeet Kune Do Concept--Unlimited Expression

The Jeet Kune Do Concept is a total concept of self-improvement. The idea is for the individual to take responsibility and develop himself or herself towards their unlimited potential. By training in the martial arts, we have a guideline for training in any other area of our life, from business to relationships. The concepts learned in your training should be transposed into your whole life experience. With this in mind, let's look at the Jeet Kune Do Concept.

The goal of Jeet Kune Do Unlimited is to develop complete martial artists. A complete martial artist is one who strives to become a great person, a great fighter, a great technician, and a great teacher. Fighting wise, this means training to be proficient in each range of combat, with or without weapons, against one or multiple, armed or unarmed opponents, in a variety of environments. Whew, sounds like alot to cover. So how do we do this without having to train ten hours a day for the next fifty years? By understanding the structure of the combative situation and adjusting our training to incorporate the entire spectrum of martial arts. Here is the logic.

Combat takes place at different distances that I have broken down into seven RANGES. There are three ranges of armed combat and four ranges of unarmed fighting. In each range you or your opponent can assume different POSTURES. The postures are broken down into six different categories. For each posture in each range you have a multitude of TECHNIQUES. The qualities that the fighter possesses that bring the techniques to life and makes them functional are called ATTRIBUTES. It is important to understand that merely being aware of the ranges, postures, techniques, and attributes is not enough. You should be interested in developing yourself into a high-performance martial artist. So how do you develop your attributes while practicing different techniques from various postures in all the ranges? *BY USING ADVANCED TRAINING METHODS!* The way you practice will determine your rate of improvement. Remember that the secret to proficiency is consistent, correct practice over a long period of time.

Efficient training methods can cut down on the time necessary for each practice session and the overall time needed to advance to higher levels of the art. If you practiced each attribute separately, each type of technique separately, each posture separately, and worked in each range separately, it would take you fifty years! Training methods can be simple and marginally efficient, or advanced and highly efficient, creating a synergistic effect on the student. An advanced drill will enhance many areas of the practitioner's repertoire and will improve the student faster than by training one area at a time. Practice as efficiently as possible to get the greatest gain out of the shortest amount of time. As you do this, be sure to keep it as fun as possible so that you will want to practice more. This way your improvement will be faster yet!

As you learn, you should do whatever you can to improve the material you gain. You may combine styles to make certain techniques more efficient or complete. You may find a better way to practice the techniques, or a clearer way to explain the art to others. Be creative. It is up to each martial artist to improve the level of the arts for the next generation.

I want each and every person who reads this book to improve him or her self beyond all expectations. Research different arts, read, experience, and learn from everyone you meet. Learn joyfully, then share joyfully. Daily improvement in every aspect of your life is the overall goal. Don't just think positively, act positively. When in doubt, remember that YOU ARE UNLIMITED!

SALUTATIONS

A salutation is one of the rituals that differentiates the Martial Arts from brawling. Here are a few of my favorites.

Jun Fan Gung Fu Salutation

1) The left hand is the scholar. He/she is intelligent, good at setting goals and making plans to reach those goals. The scholar won't get alot done if he/she doesn't act on those plans.

2) The right hand is the warrior. He/she is courageous. The warrior is great at taking action, but sometimes in the wrong direction.

3) Put the scholar and the warrior together and you have the martial artist who has the intelligence to formulate goals and plans, along with the courage it takes to consistently overcome the barriers that will arise on the journey towards the goal. The scholar/warrior will be successful because he or she will stay on course until the goal is reached.

Filipino Kali/Escrima Salutation (LaCoste System)

1) I stand before the Creator and mankind on earth.

2) I am striving for the knowledge and wisdom of the third eye, of the five senses and beyond the five senses.

3) I am striving for the love of all mankind and there will be no needless shedding of blood.

4) I bow down to you not in submission, but in respect to you .

5) I extend the hand of friendship, because I prefer it over the hand of war.

6) But if my friendship is rejected, I am trained to be a warrior with wisdom.

7) I stand in symbolism, for I serve only the Creator, my family, and my country.

8) With my mind and heart I cherish the knowledge given to me by my instructor,

9) For it is my very life in combat.

10) I am prepared to go against you even though your skill may be greater than mine.

11) Because even if my physical body should fall before you to the earth, I am not worried,

12) For I know that my spirit will arise to the heavens, as it is unconquerable.

Pentjak Silat Bukti Negara Salutation

1) I present myself to the Creator.

2) From the beginning, I present myself to the best of my ability.

3) I ask to receive from the Creator,

4) in the knowledge of the art.

5) I do receive from the Creator.

6) And those things which I do not see or under stand,

7) engrave them on my heart,

8) until the very end.

Muay Thai Salutation

The clasped hands are a sign of deep respect.

Savate

Similar to the fencing salute, it is a sign of respect.

Japanese Arts

The bow is also a sign of respect to the art, instructor, and fellow student.

SYMBOLS

Bruce Lee's Jeet Kune Do Symbol

This symbol has three parts.

1) The Yin Yang (Symbol of the Tao)

The importance of the yin yang is to show that opposites occur in nature. In essence, they must occur, for without light how would we know what darkness is? There is also an interplay between the opposites that is shown by the small circles in each half. Another interpretation is that everything is actually part of the whole; nothing is truly an independent entity.

2) The Arrows

The arrows are to emphasize that there is a dynamic interplay between the opposites. We go from one to the other all the time. We go from being awake to being asleep. We go from action to rest, or from pliable to firm. We are constantly changing.

3) The Chinese Characters

The characters say "Using no way as way, having no limitation as limitation." This is the philosophical essence of the Jeet Kune Do Concept. We use no set "way" to reach our goal, and we do not impose limitations on ourselves that will keep us from approaching our unlimited potential.

Burton Richardson's Jeet Kune Do Unlimited Symbol

The Jeet Kune Do Unlimited symbol has meaning for the martial arts and your everyday life. With diligent practice you can master the fighting arts while simultaneously gaining selfmastery.

1) The Eye

This ancient symbol is called the eye of Horus. I am using it to symbolize the Creator. Warriors of old believed that all knowledge came from the Creator through direct inspiration. This knowledge could then be passed on from person to person. New ideas that suddenly come to us are viewed as messages from the Creator.

2) Yin Yang

This is the symbol of the dualism that exists in our universe. There is positive and negative, good and bad, hard and soft, high and low, inside and outside, etc. The small circles show that there is a little of "this" in each bit of "that". Also implied is that there are two sides to everything. If you learn a technique inside the opponent's arm then there must be a way of doing the same move starting outside the arm. If you can do it with your left, you can do it with your right. When studying martial arts we must be careful not to be exclusive in our likes and dislikes. At the highest levels we should realize that being dualistic can lead to trouble. If you say that you are "for" a certain approach, you imply that you are "against" the opposite approach. When a person can transcend dualistic thinking and understand that every system or technique is useful at some time, you will no longer have to discriminate between "this" and "that". Instead, determine what works well for **YOU** in different combative situations.

3) The Daans

Daan means "path" in many Filipino dialects. This is the diagram for the paths of motion. Any motion that is made can be described by this diagram. This holds true for arm, weapon, head, body, or leg motion. At the middle of the daan is a point where all the lines connect. From this point a moving object can progress in any direction on any line, be it straight or curved. If a thrust is made with a sword towards the point, it can then move vertically, horizontally, diagonally, or in any arc away from the point. This is important to understand because it corresponds to your everyday life. No matter what you are doing now you have the choice to change directions and go wherever you heart points you. You are always at the center. Your next move is your choice and your responsibility.

4) The Arrows

The arrows symbolize a few things. Again, the warriors of old believed that all knowledge comes from the Creator down to us on Earth (first arrow). We use that knowledge while we are on the planet (second arrow). Any knowledge that we do not pass on will again go back to the Creator when we die (third arrow). The arrows also symbolize motion and therefore life itself. Anything with life has motion. Even a blade of grass will turn toward the sun to catch the life giving energy. Dead things have no motion other than the vibration of the molecules. A display of motion is essentially evidence of active changes that are constantly taking place within the living organism. Our art is much like that living body. Without change and modification the art becomes a set number of techniques with a set number of forms and drills. This is death. Combat is unlimited, the martial arts are unlimited, and, if you understand the importance of trying new approaches and developing yourself, your own abilities in the art and in life will be unlimited.

5) The Triangle

The triangle is a symbol for balance and stability. It is difficult to balance on just two points. It is the third point that allows a distribution of weight in a stable sequence. This is important to understand so that we can keep our balance while taking away an opponent's balance. In our lives it is wise to have a third point to fall back on in case the path between our first points is disrupted. The dotted lines in the triangle show that in three dimensions the figure becomes a pyramid. The pyramid is used in Pentjak Silat to describe the balance dynamics between the upper and lower body of a human being.

6) L, C, and H

There are many threesomes that are used to illustrate various relationships in the ancient art of Kali. Safety plus training skill develops fighting skill. The superconscious mind is connected to the subconscious mind which is connected to the conscious mind, and so on. The highest triangle in Kali is to have L, C, and H. That is unconditional Love for all beings (hatred towards others manifests itself in self-hate), Compassion for your fellow beings (putting yourself in another's place to feel the circumstances and pressures that cause their behavior), and Humility (regardless of how much we attain, there is always much, much more to learn and we are always below the Creator).

JEET KUNE DO UNLIMITED PHILOSOPHY

1) Look for the Truth!!!

2) The highest aspiration is to develop love, compassion and humility toward all beings.

3) We can all change and improve.

4) We can't fail unless we quit striving toward our goal. You are the only one who can say "I quit!" We are utterly relentless in the pursuit of our goals.

5) We always have a positive attitude and expect the best outcome from any situation. Always optimistic and thankful.

6) No limits; using no way as way, having no limitations as limitation.

7) The individual is more important than any style. This develops a self-empowering attitude.

8) We keep our ego in check. What we know about our selves is more important than what someone else may think or say about us.

9) The secret to proficiency is consistent, correct practice over a long period of time.

10) We are polite and friendly to all people from a position of strength until we are forced to act.

11) Our martial goal is to be functional in each range of combat, with or without a weapon, against one or more armed or unarmed assailants, in a variety of environments.

JEET KUNE DO UNLIMITED
FIGHTING PHILOSOPHY/TACTICS

1) Think in terms of totality. We can't assume that certain things will happen in real combat. There are no rules.

2) An attack executed with speed, style (efficient technique), and surprise is nearly impossible to defend against. (From Dr. M. Gi, Burmese bando)

3) The ability to read an attack will nullify the surprise, and provide the time to deal with the speed and choose a counter for the technique. (Dr. Gi)

4) Action is faster than reaction.

5) We never·turn away from aggressive people because we have developed the strength to look them in the eyes.

6) Always expect a weapon, even if you don't see one.

7) Always expect more opponents to jump into a fight.

8) Always expect the opponent to charge.

9) Train to attack and defend primary targets primarily.

Always expect a weapon

10) Look for ways to enhance our attributes while diminishing those of the opponent.

11) Hit hard, hit fast, hit first.

12) If a maneuver fails, keep your balance and hit, hit, hit, until another opportunity arises.

13) Five ways of attack
   a) Single direct attack
   b) Attack by combination
   c) Immobilization attack
   d) Attack by drawing
   e) Progressive indirect attack

14) Three ways of defense
   a) Passive
   b) Aggressive
   c) Intercepting

WAYS OF ATTACK AND DEFENSE

The concepts of attacking and defending, the essence of physical martial arts, can be described as follows.

FIVE WAYS OF ATTACK

An attack can be any offensive maneuver such as a strike, throw, lock, grab, tackle, etc.

1) Single Direct Attack- This is any attack initiated by itself. No faking or follow-ups.

2) **Attack By Combination**- This is a series of attacks launched in succession.

3) **Immobilization Attack**- Any attack that includes restricting the motion of the opponent's limbs, head, or body as part of the strategy for success.

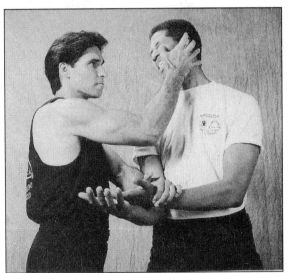

4) **Attack By Drawing-** By leaving a certain target unguarded and seemingly vulnerable, you entice an opponent to use an attack that you are prepared to counter.

5) **Progressive Indirect Attack**- This is where your attack starts towards one target and changes course mid-flight to connect with an unguarded target. The attack never back-tracks. It progresses indirectly to the target.

THREE WAYS OF DEFENSE

Before we get to the three ways of defense, you should know that there are three possible responses to an attack directed towards you.

1) You evade the attack.

2) You physically block the attack.

3) The attack is successful. (You get hit, thrown, locked.)

For self-defense purposes, we are obviously more concerned about #1 and #2! It is important not to ignore #3, though, because this will happen in real fighting.

The three ways of defense are: 1) **Passive**-Evade or block opponent's attack, then attack.

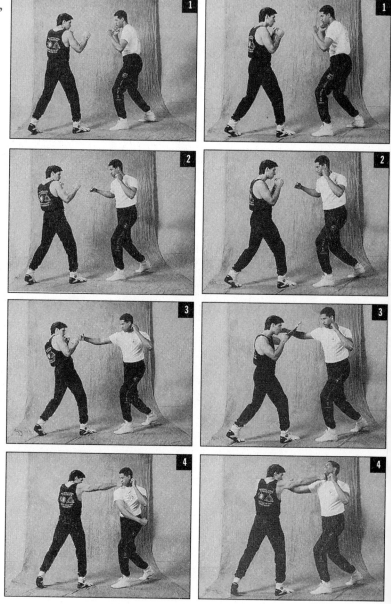

2) **Aggressive**- Attack while evading or blocking the opponent's attack.

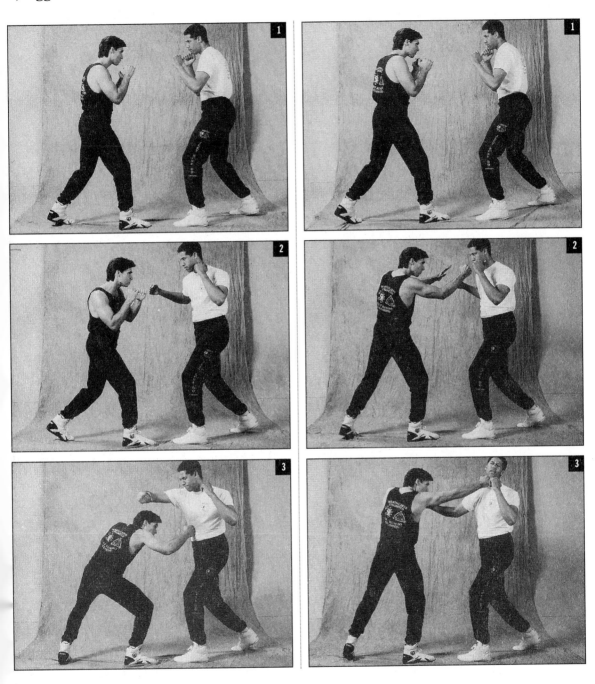

3) **Interception**- Attack on the opponent's preparation to attack, then evade or block if necessary.

These are sometimes referred to as the three timings; countering after, during, or before the opponent's attack.

WEAPONRY TRAINING A— J.K.D.C. ESSENTIAL

Zulu Stickfighting

To follow the J.K.D. Concept of martial arts training you must become proficient with weapons. This includes impact weapons, edged weapons, throwing weapons, and projectile weapons. This *doesn't* mean that you must know how to operate a surface to air missile. Our scope here is to become familiar with the most practical of common weapons.

You should know how to handle firearms. Even if you are opposed to their use, knowledge of their workings will give you an advantage if you must defend yourself against a firearm. Do you know how to tell if a revolver is loaded when it is pointing at you? Can you tell if a gunman forgot to take the safety off his semi-automatic weapon? These simple things and many more will be learned by understanding firearms. If you aren't comfortable with these weapons, find an expert to instruct you in the safe handling and usage of firearms. You should at least be able to recognize when someone is handling a gun hazardously. This could save you or others from an accidental shooting.

For those of you who want to learn how to handle a firearm, take a tactical course from a reputable instructor. While it is good to know how to stand, take aim, adjust your

breathing, then slooooooowly pull the trigger so you hit that bulls-eye, you may not have that much time in a combat situation. Target shooting is like standing still, getting your feet set, aiming your jab, then with great deliberation, throwing that jab towards the target. Guess what? If that target is alive and aggressive, it isn't going to wait for you to get ready! Learn how to shoot just like you fight; efficiently against an uncooperative opponent. Find a good instructor and he or she will help you.

As far as edged and impact weapons go, you will not be prepared to defend against them if you do not understand their capabilities and limitations. You must train well with a variety of weapons so that you will be able to defend against the same type of weapons. This will also give you the street smarts to improvise weapons and use them efficiently. Some say that you will never have a stick on the street, but there are often objects nearby that can be used the same way. Maybe you have an umbrella. When you are older you may use a cane. Others say that the only benefit to stick training is to enhance empty hand attributes, because you will never get in an actual stick fight. I have seen a stick fight at the corner of Adams and Vermont in Los Angeles. (Others who live around there won't be too surprised!) If either person knew anything about stick fighting, he would have won easily.

Another benefit to weaponry training appears when you visit different cultures. If I wasn't a competent stick fighter, I would have had problems in my travels. In the Philippines, they didn't ask me to spar empty handed. It was with sticks. In a Zulu village in South Africa they didn't want to spar empty handed. We fought with sticks and shields. If I didn't understand weaponry, I wouldn't have enjoyed experiencing their fantastic fighting methods.

Don't just dismiss training with weapons because you think that you'll never use them. You will gain more insight, be more prepared for any situation, improve your attributes, and it is loads of fun! Training with weapons is part of becoming the best that you can be.

CHAPTER 2

The Art of the Jeet Kune Do Concept

If you want to be a complete and skillful martial artist, you must understand the following. Combat occurs in different RANGES. In each range there are different POSTURES. For each posture there are an unlimited number of TECHNIQUES. ATTRIBUTES are the qualities that bring techniques alive and make them functional. In order to be proficient, you must use various TRAINING METHODS that improve all of your attributes, while practicing techniques, in various postures, in all of the ranges. Training methods are the way you practice, and the secret to proficiency is to practice correctly, and consistently, over a long period of time.

RANGES

Human beings possess natural weapons, such as elbows and knees, and have devised many other weapons that are even more efficient. Each type of weapon is particularly suited for use at a certain distance from the opponent. These distances have been broken down into the ranges of combat. The ranges are important to know so that you can be sure that you are practicing in each range. It should also be clear that there is overlap in these ranges. Just because a spear was designed for throwing from 100 feet does not mean that it is ineffective at a range of 1 foot. A gun has it's greatest advantage at a distance, but it is actually more deadly at close range.

We will start at the closest range and work our way out to the greatest distances. The opponent will be standing for now, but these ranges apply regardless of posture. For the measurement of each range, we will assume the opponent is close to your height.

Empty Hand Ranges

1) Grappling Range

This is where you can reach your palm around to the back of your opponent's head. At this range everything goes. From locking, to kicking, to headbutts, to rifle butt strikes, grappling range has it all. Some systems, such as Pentjak Silat Bukti Negara, prefer this range because it is where "all guns fire". This is the range where most headbutts, elbow strikes, and chokes occur.

2) Trapping Range

This is where, with an outstretched arm, your palm can cover your opponent's ear. This is slightly outside of grappling range. This is where most trapping and standing locking occurs.

3) Punching Range

This is where, with an outstretched arm, your palm can touch your opponent's nose. This is slightly outside of trapping range. This is where most straight punches and long hooks are thrown from.

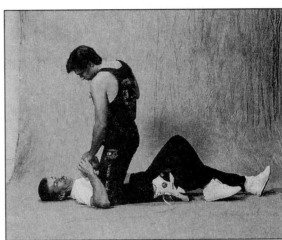

4) Kicking Range

This is where, with an outstretched arm, your fingers can't quite touch your opponent's nose. This is slightly outside of punching range. Most kicks that use the foot as the weapon are thrown from here. (Kicking with the shin can occur in trapping and punching range.)

Weaponry Ranges

This is just outside of kicking range. No empty hand tools work here, so we have to use implements which we call weapons. For clarity, let it be known that technically, a weapon is an implement that was specifically designed for combat. Other implements, such as an umbrella, are actually tools that can be used for self defense. Also be aware that short weapons, such as the knife or pocket stick, must be used inside the emptyhand ranges. The three weaponry ranges are:

1) Hand Wielded Weapons Range

This is where your rear front kick can't quite touch your opponent. You must rely on weaponry to reach the assailant. There are two types of hand wielded weapons.

a) Impact Weapons

This includes the stick, staff, tennis racket, umbrella, rock, etc. These are used to strike with.

b) Edged Weapons

Any weapon with a cutting edge. Includes the knife, sword, axe, etc. Very different than impact weapons. These are used to cut and thrust. The targets are different and defense strategy must be radically altered.

2) Throwing Weapons Range

This is just outside of where you can reach an opponent with a hand wielded weapon. Throwing weapons are used to injure or distract an opponent. They include throwing knives, spears, darts, coins, your jacket, dirt, etc.

3) Projectile Weapons Range

Most projectile weapons are still effective outside the range of throwing weapons, but are obviously very effective at closer ranges as well. They are similar to the throwing weapon, but a mechanism is used to propel the damaging object. Projectile weapons include firearms, bow and arrow, blow gun, etc.

Remember again that most tools that are effective in outer ranges can be used in the closer ranges. On the other hand, if you catch an opponent's kick, you are grappling in kicking range! Remember also that the ranges can be passed through very quickly, so the more ranges you are comfortable in the better.

An important tactic is to try to maintain the range that you favor. If a boxer can stay in punching range against a kicker, he will probably do well. The kicker will have the advantage if he can keep the boxer out at kicking range. This is why some fighters who work in just one range are successful in streetfights. They can get to and stay in the range where their system

works the best. Just be aware that it takes a high level of skill to keep an aggressive opponent from closing on you.

Another fact to remember is that the grappling range is the easiest range to maintain. You can keep an unwilling opponent there by grabbing him and not letting him escape. This is why grapplers do so well in one on one tournaments. Once they make it into grappling range it is hard for an opponent to get away. If you are not proficient in each range then you are severely limited. Even if you do well in most of the ranges, there is no reason to have a hole in your fighting arsenal. Evaluate yourself and dedicate some time to working on your weakest area. Training your best tools is always more fun, but becoming a more complete fighter is very gratifying.

POSTURES

In each range a person can assume a variety of postures. These can be used by design for mobility, deception, or defense, or they can be happenstance when a person falls, is knocked down, or is attacked while sitting, lying, etc. Even if you prefer not to fight out of certain postures, you should be familiar with them so that no one can use techniques from those postures against you. You never know when you may inadvertently end up in one of these positions as well.

1) STANDING- In an upright position with one or both feet on the ground.

2) SQUATTING- Crouching or squatting, usually with both feet on the ground and occasionally with one or both hands on the ground.

3) KNEELING- One or both knees in contact with the ground.

4) SITTING- Buttocks in contact with the ground. Legs can be extended in front, crossed in front, or crossed underneath. Also, when in a chair.

5) LYING- When your back, side, or chest is in contact with the ground.

6) HANDSTAND- When you support your body with one or two hands in contact with the ground.

TECHNIQUE

First off, realize that there are an infinite number of martial art techniques. I have heard some martial artists brag about knowing 7000 techniques. In reality, that is a very small number when you understand how to put motions together. Allow me to give a lesson in simple combination theory from the science of mathematics. This will get complicated, but stay with me.

Say I do a hand technique from Kali called the 3-count. If I block a right punch from the inside, moving my arms horizontally, the first two motions can be a right inward parry, a left outward check, and the third is a right backhand hit to the temple. That is one technique. That third hit could just as easily gone to eight other targets, namely, the eyes, nose, throat, neck, collarbone, biceps, ear, or jaw. Many other targets are available, but let's stick with those. So now we have nine techniques, the first to the temple, plus eight more. What if we change the motion slightly to allow the second hand motion to strike those nine targets instead of just checking? This means that now the second and third motions will both

hit the various targets. If the second motion went to the biceps, the third motion could go to the any of the nine targets. If the second motion went to the eyes, the third motion could go to any of the nine targets. So, we have 9 targets for the second motion times 9 for the third motion which equals 81 techniques, plus the first 9 we did earlier for a grand total of 90 techniques. Now, after each of those 90 entries, I could go to a wrist lock, arm lock, arm bar, foot sweep from the outside, foot sweep from the inside, back sweep outside, back sweep inside, choke, hair grab, right knee, left knee, right kick, left kick, right elbow, left elbow, etc., etc., etc. That is just 15 of the hundreds of places we can go after the entry. So how many techniques do we have now? 90 X 15 = 1,350 techniques. (Not to mention the first 90 we already had.)

Now, if we can do these techniques inside the right punch, we can do them outside the left punch. 1,350 X 2 = 2,700 techniques. If I reverse the direction of the motion, I can do the same techniques on the outside of the right punch and on the inside of the left, so it is actually 1,350 X 4 = 5,400 techniques. Now every time I add one new variable to the combination, we must add another 5,400 techniques. If I add a head butt at the end, we have another 5,400 techniques. If I add a fake before the combo I have another 5,400. So now we have 5,400 X 3 = 16,200 techniques. Remember how I said that we could do the 3-count entry horizontal? What if I made the first motion upward or downward? What if the second motion was upward or downward? What if the third motion was either upward or downward? That is another 6 X 16,200 techniques = 97,200 techniques. How about the diagonal upward or the diagonal downward for each motion? There is another 6 X 16,200 = 97,200 plus our previous 97,200 techniques equals 194,400 techniques. Remember our 3-count entry that went inward, backhand, backhand? Another efficient variation is to go inward, backhand, inward. We can do all the previous variations with this inward, backhand, inward. So, take 194,200 X 2 = 388,800 techniques. If we add the 90 basics from the beginning we have nearly 390,00 techniques! Do you get the idea? If you do one of those techniques every minute, for eight hours every day of every week, it would take you over TWO YEARS to get through all of them once! And that is just a portion of the three-count entry possibilities for a single punch! Think of all the different defenses that you have for the various attacks. How about weaponry? How about Muay Thai kickboxing, or Wing Chun, or Kali, or Pentjak Silat, or the African Arts, or Jiu Jitsu, or whatever. As you can see, technique is unlimited. This is why it is so important to learn conceptually.

You will never be able to learn each and every technique. Instead, learning the martial arts should be like learning how to write. Learn the alphabet, then learn how to spell words, then learn how to make sentences and paragraphs and you can create as many stories as you wish. You don't learn to spell then spend the rest of your life copying stories written by other people. You get to write what you want to write, your own expression. The same is true in the martial arts. Learn the basics well and you are only bound by your imagination. If your imagination is unlimited, then you too are truly unlimited.

Unfortunately, we exist in a world where the precious commodity of time is limited. This is why it is so important to prioritize your training methods. You should learn as much as you can, but you must also be able to distinguish between those techniques that are only good for demonstration, and those which will give good results in an all-out street fight. Your training time is limited, so you must make it as efficient as possible. Always practice the basic fighting techniques using training methods that are alive first. After you have improved in each range, then if you like, take the time to play with other techniques which may improve some attributes, but which are difficult to apply against an aggressive opponent. Training the fancy methods first will lead to a martial artist who looks good when his or her partner feeds the "proper energy", but can't survive a street encounter. That is totally against the principles of Bruce Lee's Jeet Kune Do Concept.

Here is one more important tip for street-fighting. Never expect a technique to work exactly the way you want it to. If you think your elbow is definitely going to knock that guy out, you are going to throw it and wait for him to hit the deck. If he takes it and keeps coming you are may get discouraged and fall out of your game plan. Throw your shot for all you're worth and keep going. If it does work, great. Treat that as a pleasant surprise. If it doesn't, you will be mentally prepared to continue until you can end the fight the way that you want to.

ATTRIBUTES

Attributes are the abilities that we possess that enhance our performance. These are the qualities that bring techniques alive and make them functional. The great thing about attributes is that each one can be improved through proper training. If you are not fast, do speed drills. If you are not strong, try weight training and calisthenics. Identify your weakest areas and and work daily to improve them.

1) HEALTH- Without health your martial arts knowledge is useless. Proper mental focus, diet, training, and rest are imperative.

2) MOBILITY- The ability to move your body. From arm motions, to footwork, to head movements, your mobility is crucial to your martial arts skill. Those who have paralysis or loss of limbs should enhance the mobility of the rest of their body.

3) ATTITUDE- Your attitude determines how you approach a conflict and how you approach life. It is your choice to be optimistic or pessimistic. In an altercation you can be bold and aggressive or timid and fearful. It is important to train your attitude just as you do any other attribute. You should be able to go into a directed rage at a moments notice, then regain your calm immediately.

4) FLOW- The ability to change a failure into success by altering your path is flow. When a technique is foiled, work from there to create another technique and another until you succeed.

5) TIMING- The ability to have your technique implemented when it is most likely to work is good timing. An opening may occur for just a fraction of a second. It is up to you to judge when to initiate an action so that it lands while the window of opportunity is open.

6) POWER- This is the ability to transfer force. The more weight you have, the less velocity that is needed. The lighter you are, the faster you must move your body. Developing good power is important because your blow does not have to be as accurate to be effective.

7) SPEED- The ability to deliver an action quickly, and with great acceleration. The greater your speed the easier it will be to time your attack. Even if you are a little late initiating your offense, high speed will compensate for the error and you will still be successful.

8) ACCURACY- The ability to place your weapons in the location you desire. If you have great speed, timing, and power, but your accuracy is awful, you will not achieve the desired affect. You must hit your goal to get results.

9) COORDINATION- The ability to move different parts of your body independently of the others while maintaining grace and rhythm.

10) SENSITIVITY- The ability to sense your surroundings. In martial arts we primarily rely on visual, tactile, and aural sensitivity. The ability to see an opponent's position or read his intent while not in contact is visual. The ability to feel an opponent's position or intent is tactile. The ability to hear an opponent's position or intent is aural. This is very important to develop so that you can always be at least one step ahead of the opponent.

11) RHYTHM- The ability to move in sequence at a steady pace. Rhythm is important for ease of movement, disguising attacks, and enhancing speed and power. You must also know how to throw off your opponent's rhythm by altering your own.

12) STRENGTH- The ability to generate a great amount of force. Strength does matter! Increasing your strength will enhance every aspect of your martial arts skill.

13) ENDURANCE- The ability to maintain a high level of exertion over a period of time. The last thing you should have to worry about in a real altercation is your cardiovascular conditioning. This should not enter into the equation. If you get tired all of your other attributes will be adversely affected.

14) FLEXIBILITY- The ability to move your body to the skeletal limits without being hampered by shortened muscles, ligaments, or tendons. Flexibility will enhance your movement and give you an extra advantage in grappling situations.

15) BALANCE- The ability to maintain a position of relative stability when stationary or mobile, thus being able to easily change direction at will. Balance is an important part of many of the other attributes such as power, speed, and coordination.

16) DURABILITY- The ability to absorb punishment without adverse affect. This is good old toughness. Not something we want to employ, but often we have no choice. Sparring is great for developing this important quality.

17) AGILITY- The ability to change direction quickly. The agile fighter tends to have great speed and mobility.

18) KNOWLEDGE- The information that you have absorbed through different methods of learning and experience. This enhances flow by giving you more options to flow to.

19) EXPERIENCE- The insights gained through actually trying the arts. Experiencing hard-core Muay Thai training enhances your skill much more than watching a video of training. Practicing drills is a different experience than an all-out brawl. Hard sparring experience will cultivate the calm demeanor that is necessary in a tough situation. If you lose your composure, you will lose your technique.

20) RELAXATION- The ability to stay calm and allow your mind and muscles to work properly while under great stress. Tension slows reflexes, execution of technique, and your ability to think and flow. It also disrupts spiritual alignment.

21) PRECISION- The ability to perform a movement with exactness and efficiency at every increment of the motion. Being in control at all times.

TRAINING METHODS

Training methods are the various ways that we can practice to improve our skills. The simple drills can isolate one technique or attribute while advanced training methods can incorporate many of the aspects of the martial arts. It is important to remember that drilling is not the same as all-out fighting. Just because you are good at a sensitivity drill like Chi Sao doesn't mean that you are a great fighter. Just because you are fast and powerful on the Thai pads doesn't mean that you will do well in a Thai Boxing match. Even sparring, one of the most advanced training methods, is just a drill, and drills are not street combat.

I have broken the training methods into three major categories. In each category your training will either be "set", in other words predetermined, or "free" with little predetermined structure. Be sure that your training sessions include all of the ranges, postures, and attributes that we have covered. Since the amount of techniques are infinite, you will have to decide which ones you spend your time on. Just remember to first practice the most probable responses before going on to the more complex scenarios. When two people fight, the one with the stronger asics usually wins, so work those basics hard! Also employ the different tactics that we have discussed. Each type of training should be done empty handed and with the weaponry. Remember, SAFETY FIRST!! IF YOU HURT YOURSELF TRAINING YOU WON'T BE ABLE TO IMPROVE!!

CATEGORY 1 • Solo Training

This is when you practice by yourself. You won't always have access to a partner, so it is important to take the initiative yourself and improve. When you practice solo, you either do your motions in the air or on equipment. Here is how you can break this down.

1) Training In The Air

a) <u>Form Training</u> (set)

Practicing set forms are good for developing the different attributes, and practicing your techniques. They are especially good for the beginner who may not be sure what to practice.

b) <u>Shadow Boxing</u> (free)

This is done in the air and is free. There is no pattern, just your own self-expression. Remember to use all of your techniques. People will often restrict themselves to kickboxing when they hear the term shadow boxing.

2) Equipment Training

Any training done using an apparatus of some sort to improve your skills.

a) <u>Form training</u> (set) You may do a prescribed drill over and over again to get the motions ingrained. You may do what is called the 1,2 series on a heavy bag. You jab, cross, then follow with a kick from either leg, either elbow, or either knee. If it is a set routine, then it is considered a form.

b) <u>Free training</u> (free) Doing whatever comes naturally on the heavy bag, Wing Chun dummy, tire, or any other training device you have.

3) Visualization

This is where you use your imagination to practice. Be sure to imagine with all of your senses. See the attacker, hear the attacker, feel the intensity, smell the surroundings, taste whatever is in your mouth. Imagine the biggest, toughest, meanest opponent you can. See yourself dominating him. Next, see him taking your best shots and smashing you around, but you refuse to give in and ultimately prevail. Imagine every circumstance possible, but always have one ending; you as the victor!

CATEGORY 2 • With a Partner

Each training method described here should be done in every range, against one or more opponents, both empty hand and with weapons. There are three categories of training methods when working with a partner or partners; Two or more person Forms, Drills, and Sparring. These are listed as 1, 2, and 3 respectively.

1) Two Or More Person Form

Any set pattern done with a partner where all of the moves are predetermined.

2) Drills

All of the following drills can be done two ways.

a) On Your Partner

When using your partner, control should be used to avoid injury. Be sure to practice accuracy by always attacking precisely towards the actual target.

b) On Equipment Held By Your Partner.

When using equipment, you can blast as hard as you like. Use the following drilling concepts when using focus gloves, Thai pads, the kicking shield, body armor, or whatever other types of impact equipment you use. Just remember that the equipment is rarely held exactly where the target actually would be.

Next comes the three structures of drilling; Abecedario, Sumbrada, and a combination of the two. (I use the Pilipino terms out of respect.) Practice both on a partner and with equipment to get all of the benefits of the various structures.

1) *Abecedario*

This is where only one person feeds attacks and the other person defends and counter-attacks. Be sure to practice all three ways of defense. The baseball analogy is batting practice; one person pitches and the other gets to do all of the hitting.

a) Set
This is where you know what is to be fed, and there is a specific response for each feed.

b) Free
Either the feed is set and the counter is free, or the feed free and the counter is set, or both the feed and the counter are free.

2) Sumbrada

This is counter for counter. The baseball analogy is playing catch. You throw one to me, I catch it, and I throw one back to you. In martial arts terms, you attack me, I counter it and attack you, you counter that and we repeat the process.

a) Set

This is where all attacks and counters are predetermined.

b) Free

This is where each attack and counter is spontaneous, nothing is set except the parameters of the drill.

3) Combine Abecedario and Sumbrada

You can combine the two basic drills by having one person attack while the other person defends and does a series of counter-attacks. Sometime in the course of the counter-attacks, the first person counters and begins a series of counter-attacks and so on.

a) Set

Each move is predetermined.

b) Free

The attacks and counters are spontaneous. The number of attacks before a new counter may be predetermined.

These are the three structures of drills. Each of these drills can then be enhanced by inserting cues. This turns the training method into a "cue drill".

CUE DRILLS

To take the techniques you practice in the training methods and make them become a natural response when you are under pressure, you should practice CUE DRILLS. This way you will train yourself to actually respond to the opponent's energy rather than just going through the drill by rote. It is very easy to get so familiar with a drill that you end up repeating a memorized pattern instead of feeling and responding. These drills are exciting to practice as they require your full concentration. Each of the drills that I have previously outlined, with or without a partner, can be modified and performed as a cue drill.

A cue is a certain stimulus to which you will respond. During the course of a drill, the cue will be given. You will then respond appropriately. If the response is predetermined, we call it a "set" cue drill. If the response just depends on your flow, then it is a "free" cue drill.

An example could be that during focus glove training your partner will suddenly throw a big overhand right at you. That is the cue. A set response may be to bob and weave and go back to hitting. Every time your partner throws that right hand, you bob and weave and continue hitting. A free response would be where you just respond depending on where you are at the time. It depends on your balance, what you are throwing at the time, and how soon you recognize the punch coming in. You might block and hit at the same time. You may enter inside and throw your partner. If the timing is right, you may bob and weave like on the set drill. The response is up to you. This develops split second timing and the ability to evaluate and respond to an attack in an efficient manner. The ultimate cue drill is where you have no idea what your partner is going to attack you with, and you must do whatever you can to be successful. This brings us to the next category of training methods, sparring.

3) SPARRING

Sparring is absolutely essential, but it is just a drill. It is a great drill that can simulate street situations, but it is still just a drill. Often people who become proficient at sparring think that they are invincible on the street, even though their gym sessions are replete with rules and regulations. Sparring must be restricted, because without safety factors you won't survive the training! The Filipino arts have developed great training methods out of necessity. They couldn't pull out the blades and just spar. Drills had to be developed to simulate combat. Thai boxers don't go hard when they spar. If they did, they would be too beaten up to perform at their best in the actual bout. There should always be restrictions, but be sure to change the rules occasionally and spar in every range. Spar safely and you will improve faster than you thought possible. Here are the types of sparring that you should experience.

a) *Isolated*

This is where you isolate certain tools. Maybe you just use the jab for a round. Maybe you isolate the lead leg and the rear punch. It is a good way to progress to the more free forms of sparring without being overwhelmed. If you are experienced, but are getting hit with the same tool all of the time, isolate it and work on countering that particular tool.

b) *Long Range*

This is where you spar at a distance without any contact. This trains your visual awareness to look for holes in your partner's defense, while countering full speed attacks. The drawback is that you are not working your sense of distance at all.

c) *Light Contact, with protective equipment*

Put on protective equipment and spar lightly. Remember that "light" doesn't mean slow. You can still use speed if you both have the proper control. Sparring light is important because you get the benefits of sparring without having to go to work the next day with a black eye or a split lip.

d) Light Contact, little protective equipment

This will give you more ease of movement, and you will feel more when you get hit. Pain is a great motivator, so use it to your advantage.

e) Heavy Contact, protective equipment

This is whole different ball-game. The dynamics of fighting change when a person is trying to lay in shots with power. Whether it is kickboxing, grappling, or stickfighting, sparring with heavy contact will change your outlook on training. Only do this in the presence of a qualified instructor who has been trained to administer first aid. Wearing protective equipment does not mean that you won't be hurt!

f) Heavy Contact, little protective equipment

The final test of sparring. This is where you rely solely on your skills to protect you. This is only recommended for those who have plenty of experience sparring hard with protective equipment. While painful, this type of sparring will allow you to make the other types more realistic. Only do this in the presence of a qualified instructor who has been trained to administer first aid.

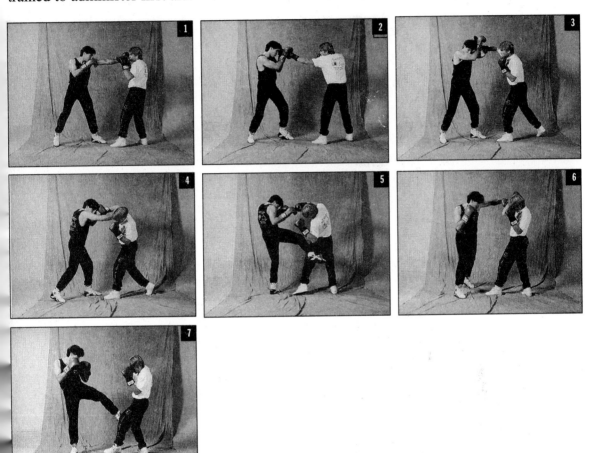

That is the outline for training with a partner. Using these methods will allow you to work hard while working smart to gain the greatest possible results from your training.

CATEGORY 3 • Spiritual

This is the last category of training methods, and is one that is kept secret by many and overlooked by most. This is where you enlist the help of the spiritual realm for guidance, knowledge, understanding, or influence in your life. Some people look at this as "taboo" or "evil", but this is what every religion in the world is based upon; the information that was handed down from the Creator, whatever name is given Him/Her. What good is a religion if a person in that religion can't make contact with the next realm? If you haven't developed the ability yourself, it is wise to ask a more "connected" person to help you. This can be a priest, a rabbi, a caliph, a yogi, a kahuna, or whatever you want to call a person who is in touch with the spiritual realm. There are two ways to receive divine guidance.

1) Direct communication (Prayer, Meditation)

The actual communication can be set, as in a written prayer, affirmation, or meditation, or free, coming straight from your heart. I've put them in four categories.

1- You ask for others   2- You ask for yourself

3- Have someone else ask for others   4- Have someone else ask for you

2) Dreams/ Visions

This is where a vision comes to you and you observe and learn from it. You may also participate in the vision. There are countless martial artists who have gained insight through this type of training. I personally know of many who have benefitted in this manner. You should be open to this method too.

While this isn't a book on spirituality, I think it is important for each individual to keep things in perspective. The only thing we know in a real street fight is that the aggressor wants to hurt us. We don't know if there are others lurking in the shadows, if weapons will be involved, if the thug wants money or our life. This is why we prepare so thoroughly. The one thing we know about life is that each of us will die. It is important to prepare for that as well. I would advise you to use the J.K.D. Concept. Research and experience for yourself.

CHAPTER 3
Examples of the Jeet Kune Do Concept

The techniques that follow are possible combinations that can occur out of flow. These are not meant to give the impression that if a person throws a side kick you simply do A,B,C,D,E,F, every time. Real combat is a constantly changing dynamic of energy that you must feel and relate to spontaneously.

I have borrowed from many different arts in putting these techniques together. I have borrowed from Jun Fan Gung Fu, Wing Chun, Kali, Escrima, Arnis, Pentjak Silat, Muay Thai, Savate, Shoot Wrestling, Japanese Jiu Jitsu, Brazilian Jiu Jitsu, African arts, Shaolin Kenpo Karate, and others. I respect each in their own right, as they can all be effective fighting styles, depending upon the skill of the practitioner.

Technique 1   Knee counter

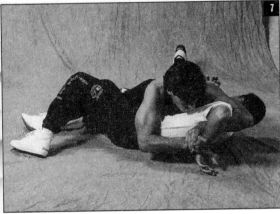

1 Ready position.

2 As the opponent delivers a rear knee, Burton sidesteps and parries the knee while pushing the chest to off balance the assailant.

3 Burton continues the parry into a catch, and checks the rear hand,

4 and turns to throws the opponent.

5 Burton drops his body across the opponent,

6 grabs the wrist,

7 and ends with an arm lock.

Technique 2   **Elbow counter**

1 Ready

2 Burton stops the elbow with his left hand before it reaches full power,

3 raises the opponent's arm with the right arm,

4 and torques the right hand outward to off balance the opponent,

5 while stepping in behind the lead foot.

6 Burton sweeps the foot,

7 then stomps the ankle to keep the opponent down.

Technique 3 — Trapping to throwing to locking

This technique is straight from Pentjak Silat Bukti Negara.

1 Ready

2 Burton traps the punch,

3 and throws a right which is blocked.

4 Burton threads his left hand through the other side to hit the face,

and retraps with his left while palming the face.

6 He tilts the head back while squeezing the mandible,

7 and steps deep behind the opponent's leg.

8 Burton turns and backsweeps,

9 for a hard fall,

10 which culminates in a wrist lock.

Technique 4   **Simple defense and throw**

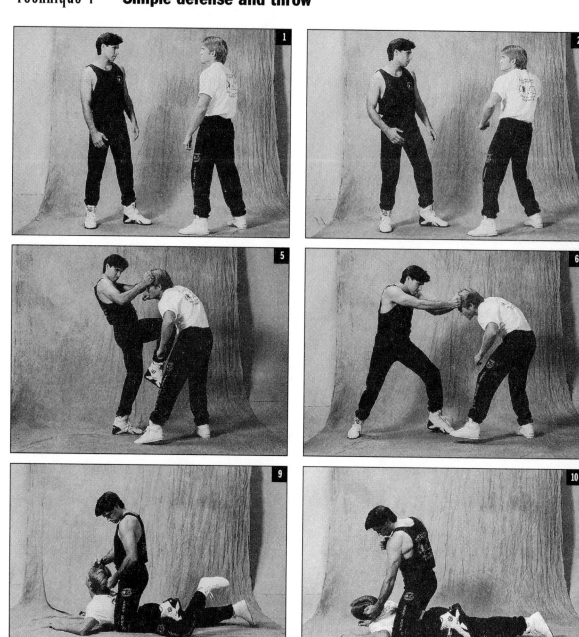

 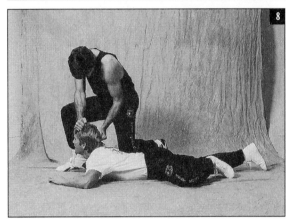

Ready

As the opponent prepares to punch,

Burton dives in with a double palm strike to the face, (Intercepting)

grabs the hair with both hands,

and throws a strong knee.

Burton steps back,

and drags the opponent to the ground.

Burton kneels on the back,

mounts the back,

and has the assailant's full attention.

Technique 5   Kick and punch counter

1   Ready

2   Burton parries the front kick from the inside,

3   and pulls to off balance the opponent.

4   He parries the cross from the outside,

5   while preparing to throw,

6   a kick to the groin.

Technique 6 **Trapping Range to Kicking Range**

Ready

As the opponent prepares to strike, Burton traps and punches. (Intercepting)

He traps both hands to pull the opponent into a head butt,

then puts both hands on the forearms,

to push the opponent,

out to range for a side kick to the head.

Technique 7 Trapping to Elbows to Sweeping

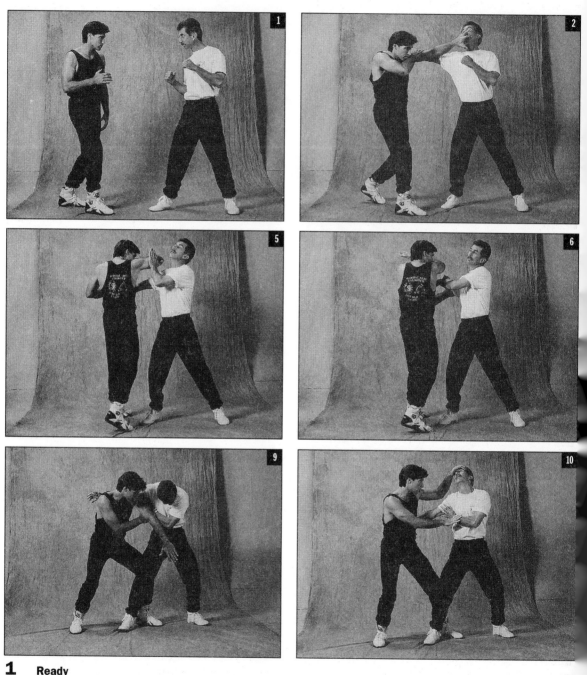

1 Ready

2 Burton enters inside the jab to parry and claw the face simultaneously. (Aggressive)

3 He turns and delivers an upward elbow strike,

4 then prepares for a,

5 back elbow which is blocked.

6 Burton grabs the blocking arm,

7   and lands the back elbow.

8   He retraps as he turns and steps behind the opponent's lead foot to deliver a left elbow,

9   and a palm strike to the groin.

10 He tilts the opponent's head back while maintaining the hand trap,

11 & 12 and finishes by sweeping the opponent.

Technique 8 **Trapping to Grappling**

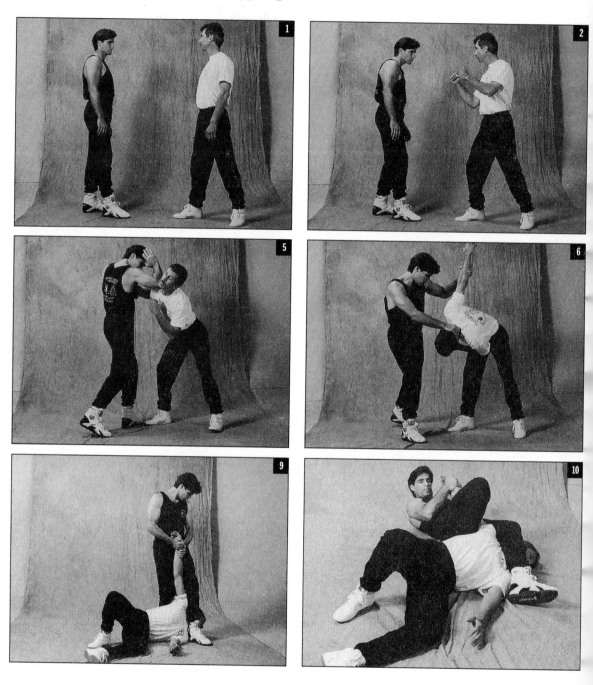

1 Ready

2 The opponent gets aggressive,

3 so Burton traps both hands, (Intercepting)

4 knees the groin,

5 elbows the neck,

6 and goes into a throw,

7 to land the opponent,

8 on his side. Burton maintains a grasp of the opponent's arm, and kicks the jaw,

9 which puts him in position to,

10 sit down into an armbar.

Technique 9 **Hair grab to Throw.**

1   Ready

2   Burton decides to take the initiative by throwing a knee which the opponent blocks with both hands.

3   This leaves the opponent's head unprotected. Burton delivers a double ear slap,

4   grabs the hair, twists the head to the side,

5   and knees the jaw.

6   Burton continues the twisting motion,

7   grabs the opponent's chin, and kneels to set up for,

8   a very hard throw.

9   Burton follows up by pinning the opponent.

Technique 10   Sitting Posture to Attack By Drawing

1 Burton sits in a crossed legged posture so that his head appears vulnerable to a kick.

2 The opponent takes the bait and aims a kick at Burton's head.

3 Burton checks the kick with his right and grabs the leg with his left while leaning forward to diminish the power of the kick.

4 Burton moves forward as he stands with the leg in his arms,

5 and tosses the unsuspecting attacker.

Technique 11   Fakes to Kick Entry to Throw and Lock

1   Ready outside of kicking range.

2   To confuse the opponent, Burton fakes low,

3   fakes high,

4   then has his opening to kick the groin.

5   He moves in with a trap and palm strike,

6   and pushes the head to give space,

to move in and set up for,

a back sweep.

Burton follows the opponent to the ground,

and pins the opponent with his body while preparing,

to apply a wrist and shoulder lock.

Burton finishes with an elbow strike.

Technique 12 Kick Combination

1. **Ready**

2. **Burton stop kicks the opponent's rear round house kick. (Intercepting)**

3. **and rechambers for,**

4. **a roundhouse kick, to the groin.**

5. **Burton rechambers once more,**

6. **for a side kick to the head.**

Technique 13   **Trapping Range to Grappling**

1   Ready

2   Burton fakes a low jab, which is blocked.

3   He traps with his left while disengaging his right,

4   for an ear slap. This is blocked also,

5   so Burton tries to punch with his left, but to no avail.

6   Trapping isn't working, so Burton changes ranges by,

7   dropping to the ground, while putting his left foot outside the opponent's lead foot and pulling inside the lead leg,

8   to take the opponent to the ground.

9   The opponent falls where he is susceptible to,

10   a right kick to the chin.

Technique 14   Defense Against an Ambush

 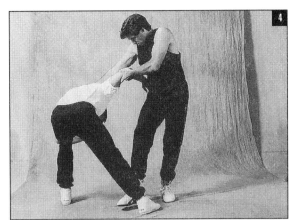

1 Burton is lucky that the opponent grabs the shoulder before punching.

2 Burton raises his arm and turns to release the grab and protect him from the punch.

3 This also puts him in position to move in, trap the arm and neck,

4 and sweep.

5 The opponent doesn't go all the way down, so Burton stomps to the back of his leg,

6 grabs his hair,

7 and pulls the head back in preparation for,

8 a forearm strike to the throat.

Technique 15 **Kick Defense**

1 Ready

2 The opponent throws a lead roundhouse kick,
Burton uses his knee to strike the nerve
inside the leg. (Aggressive)

3 The opponent steps back,

4 and fires a right roundhouse kick.

5 Burton anticipates the kick, and
throws a stomp kick to the support leg while
blocking. (Aggressive)

6 This topples the opponent.

Technique 16 Stop Kick to Trapping to Throw and Lock or Break

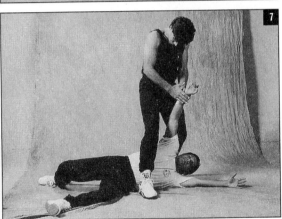 

1   Ready

2   Burton uses a stop kick as the opponent jabs. (Intercepting)

3   Burton grabs with his right hand,

4   and punches with his left.

5   Retaining the opponent's arm, Burton steps behind the lead leg while palming the face,

6   and throws the opponent.

7   Burton steps over the fallen opponent,

8   and kneels on his neck,

9   while entwining the arm,

10   for the lock or break.

Technique 17 Interception to Throw and Lock or Break

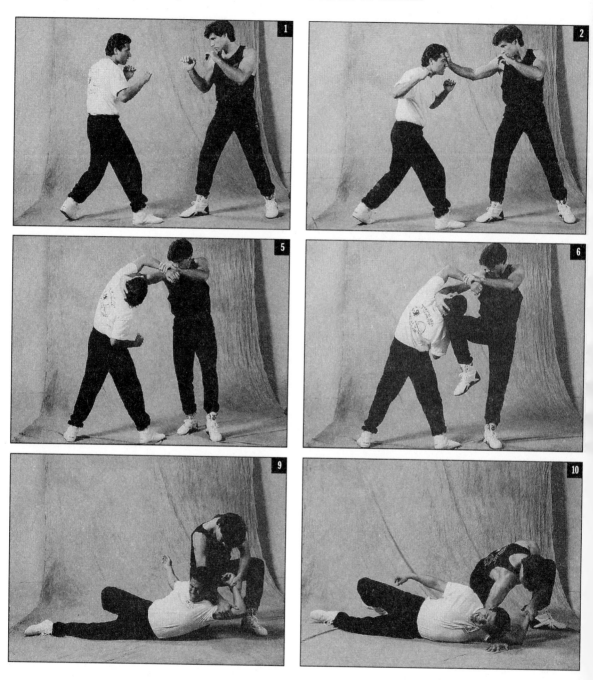

1 Ready

2 As the opponent prepares to punch, Burton palms the face (Interception),

3 and moves his hand to thumb the eye.

4 Burton catches the opponent's arm,

5 and uses the position,

6 to knee the head,

7 and spin the opponent.

8 Burton quickly repositions his right arm so that his forearm is behind the neck and his hand is inside the biceps.

9 Burton continues the throw,

10 that ends in a neck crank along with an arm lock or break.

Technique 18   Defense Against a Tackle

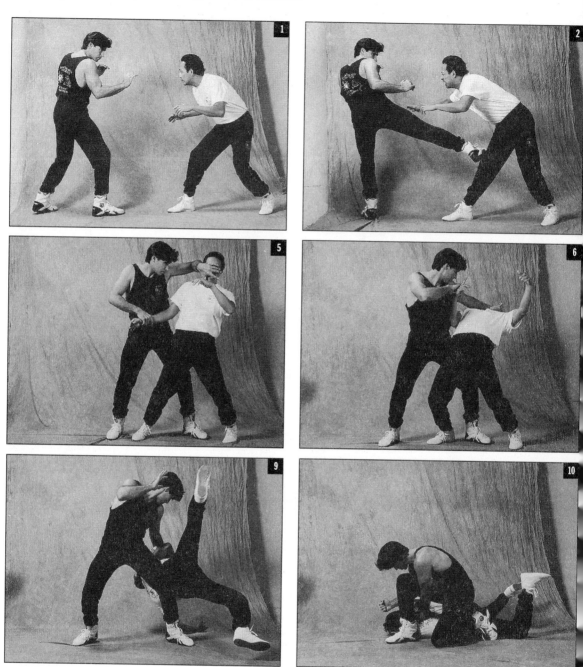

1   The opponent crouches, ready to rush.

2   Burton stops him with a low side kick, (Intercepting)

3   then palms the face while trapping the hand.

4   Burton kicks the thigh with his shin while pushing the lead shoulder. This gives him room to,

5   step in behind the opponent's leg, and palm the face,

6   which turns into a head tilt.

7   Burton hammers the groin,

8   moves in deeper, and puts his elbow on the opponent's chest to prepare for,

9   a very hard throw.

10   Burton turns and secures the opponent.

Technique 19   Defense Against a Tackle

1. The opponent prepares to rush.

2. Burton strikes at the neck and pushes the arm to keep the opponent off.

3. Burton pushes the opponent's head down and traps it,

4. under the upper arm, and hooks his right forearm under the opponent's left arm.

5. Burton turns to throw the opponent,

6. and goes down with him,

7. to use the position,

8. for a pin and neck crank.

Technique 20 **Trapping to Throwing to Neck Crank**

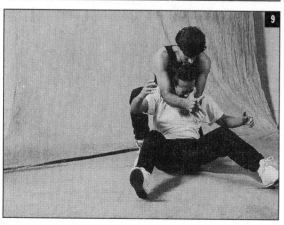

Ready position

As the jab come out, Burton parries and simultaneously checks the rear hand,

and elbows the face.

Burton places his left hand on the left side of the opponent's head,

and moves in, sliding the right arm across the throat,

and securing a hold.

He drops his weight and pulls the opponent over his leg,

for a hard fall.

Burton places his elbows on the opponent's chest,

and leans forward to crank the neck.

Technique 21   Capturing a Punch for Locking

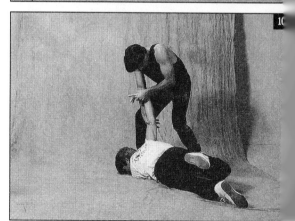

1   Ready

2   As the opponent jabs, Burton parries and slips the punch while palming the face. (Aggressive)

3   Burton cuts hard inside the opponent's arm,

4   which pulls his head into a shoulder strike.

5   Burton transfers his hands,

6   to throw the opponent with a wrist flex.

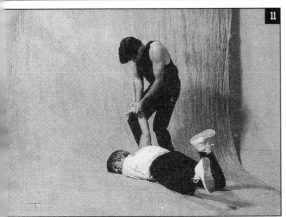
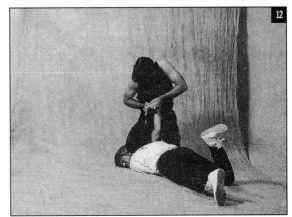

7   The opponent lands on his back, but Burton wants him face down.

8   Burton pulls the arm straight while bracing the elbow,

9   and forces the opponent,

10   onto his stomach,

11   where Burton kneels,

12   and secures the opponent with a wrist and shoulder lock.

Technique 22 **Trapping to Sweeping**

1   Ready

2   As the opponent prepares to punch, Burton moves in,

3   traps, and hits. (Intercepting) The opponent blocks the punch,

4   so Burton wedges his left hand through the opening to palm the face.

5   He moves in as he switches the left hand to a head tilt,

6   and sweeps hard.

Technique 23 Kick Entry to Throw

1 Ready

2 Burton parries the jab,

3 then throws a side kick to the thigh.

4 Burton palms the face as he moves in,

5 behind the opponent's lead leg.

6 Burton leans in with his arms across the opponent's chest,

7 and collapses the elbow for a hard throw.

8 Burton is ready in case the opponent recovers.

Technique 24   **Elbow Counter**

1 Ready

2 As the opponent starts to throw the right elbow,

3 Burton reaches in, to block the strike by grabbing the neck,

4 and returns an elbow to the face.

5 He grabs behind the neck with his right,

6 delivers a knee to the chest,

7 and continues with the same motion to kick the groin.

Technique 25 **Punching Range to Throw**

1 Ready

2 As the opponent throws the rear hook, Burton simultaneously blocks and hits. (Aggressive)

3 The opponent throws a lead hook and Burton again blocks and hits.

4 Burton moves in to lock the arm,

5 and knee the sternum.

6 From this position, he turns his body and starts,

7 a hard throw,

8 that lands the opponent on his back.

Technique 26   **Punching Range to Kicking Range**

Ready

The opponent jabs, Burton parries,

and returns a jab to the face.

Burton ducks the rear swing,

and throws a ridge hand,

to the groin.

Burton stands,

and delivers a side kick inside the knee,

& 10 that takes the opponent down.

Technique 27   Defending the Ambush

1   The opponent sneaks up, but Burton sees him.

2   Burton parries the punch and palms the face, (Aggressive)

3   to turn the opponent's head.

4   Burton elbows the biceps,

5   bends the opponents arm,

6   and throws a punch to the ribs,

7   as he secures the arm lock.

For extra security, Burton palms the face,

9   continues the motion to twist the head,

10   and completes the arm lock/neck crank combination.

Technique 28   **Defense for a Push**

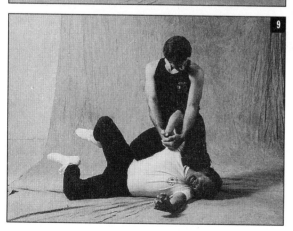

 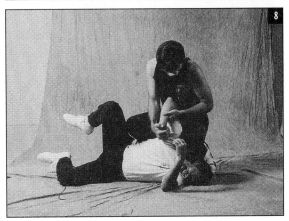

Ready

The opponent pushes.

Burton parries the arm as he strikes the biceps,

then traps the arm while throwing a back forearm to the neck.

Burton grabs the arm with both hands and steps behind the opponent's lead leg.

Burton puts weight on the arm by kneeling,

then pulls the opponent over the knee for the throw.

He controls the opponent by kneeling on his face and ribs,

and finishes with a wrist lock or break.

Technique 29   **Defense Against the Guard**

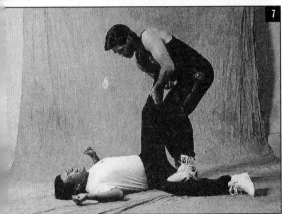
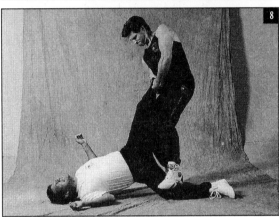

1   The opponent has Burton in his guard. Burton traps both of his arms so he can't punch or maneuver.

2   Burton stands up,

3   lifts the opponent up,

4   and slams him on the ground,

     so that he will release his legs.

5   Burton entwines the opponent's left leg,

7   steps on the right thigh,

8   and applies an Achilles' tendon lock.

Technique 30   Countering a Kick Catch

1   Ready

2   Burton throws a right front kick,

3   which the opponent catches.

4   Burton bends his leg, while palming the face,

5   grabs the opponent's right hand,

6   and pushes the face so that he can,

7   put his foot into the abdominal region,

8   which results in a lock or break,

9   and a takedown.

Technique 31 **Throwing Weapon for a Distraction**

1 An attacker approaches.

2 Burton throws his keys at the assailant,

3 and rushes in,

4 to trap both legs.

5 He lifts the opponent,

6 turns him,

7 and throws him hard to the ground.

8 Burton grabs the opponent's arm,

9 pulls up and steps over his head with the left foot,

10 steps over with the right foot, drags the opponent's head in behind his knee,

11 and kneels to squeeze the neck while applying the arm bar or break.

Technique 32   Kick Entry to Throw

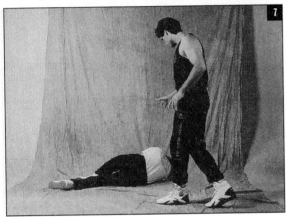

1 Ready

2 Burton intercepts the opponent with a side kick on his preparation to attack. (Intercepting)

3 Burton moves in with both hands outside the opponent's outstretched arm,

4 and tilts his head while delivering a round-house kick with the shin to the thigh.

5 Burton retains the head tilt while stepping in deep behind the opponent.

6 The opponent is thrown by pulling his head back and downward while tripping him with the leg.

7 The opponent falls in an awkward position.

Technique 33 Defense from a Relaxed Position

1   Burton doesn't seem to react to the threat.

2   As the punch comes in, Burton parries and starts,

3   an inverted roundhouse kick to the groin.

4   He grabs the wrist, steps in and,

5   punches to the head.

6   Burton presses down at the shoulder while keeping the arm taut,

7   and positions the opponent's arm for,

8   an arm bar using the abdominals,

9   along with a neck twist.

Technique 34 **Kick Defense**

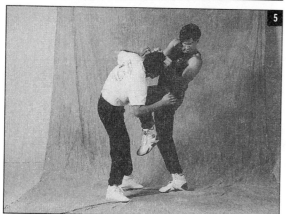

1   Ready

2   Burton parries the opponent's front kick from the inside,

3   and throws a powerful kick to the groin.

4   He moves in and grabs the hair with both hands,

5   and pulls the opponent into a knee.

6   Burton twists the opponent around,

7   and throws him to the ground. He maintains a hair hold with the left hand while winding up for,

8   a chop to the throat.

Technique 35   Fast Sweep   (ABD)

1   Burton is ready with his hands down. He hopes to draw the jab.

2   As the opponent starts to punch,

3   Burton's hands come up from the inside of the jab in a quick, pulling motion to send the opponent's arm down. This slightly off balances the opponent,

4   so that the sweep occurs easily,

5   and the opponent falls fast and hard.

Technique 36 Punching Range to Kicking Range to Trapping Range

1   Ready

2   The opponent jabs, Burton slips back with a parry,

3   then returns a jab, but the opponent has moved out of range.

4   Burton flows into a roundhouse kick to the groin,

5   then moves in to trap and palm the temple,

6   and finishes with a downward elbow.

Technique 37   **Knife Defense**

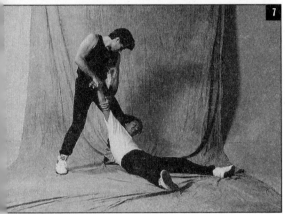

1 Burton faces the armed assailant.

2 Burton slips back out of range of the slash,

3 then quickly enters behind the knife,

4 to trap the knife arm with both hands,

5 and head butt.

6 Burton keeps a tight hold on the knife arm and sweeps.

7 He braces the assailant's head with his knee,

8 and brings the knife close to the attacker. This is often referred to as "bargaining position".

Technique 38   Knife Defense

1 Knife threat from the side.

2 As the attacker thrusts toward the midsection, Burton sidesteps and parries with his left hand,

3 and moves in to tilt the head with his right hand while retaining the check with his left.

4 Burton throws him back, bouncing him off the knee,

5 then exchanges hands. The left hand is on the face, the right grabs the wrist.

6 Burton drops his left knee on the face while locking or breaking the arm over his right thigh.

Technique 39 Defense for a Club

1   The attacker threatens with a bat.

2   As he starts to swing, Burton waits,

3   and ducks once the swing is committed toward his head.

4   As the bat goes by, Burton moves in,

5   and covers the attacker's head with a coat.

6   He continues in and positions for,

7   a back sweep.

8   Burton pins the attacker by pushing on his head and locking or breaking his arm.

Technique 40 **Two Attackers**

1 Burton is faced by two attackers.

2 As one attacker swings, Burton moves toward him,

3 and intercepts the punch by putting both hands on the attacker's face and stepping on his foot.

4 This way he throws the attacker while gaining distance from the other.

5 The second attacker approaches,

6 and throws,

7 a big right hook which Burton ducks,

8 while hitting the groin.

9 He finishes with a knee to the ribs.

Technique 41 **Three Attackers**

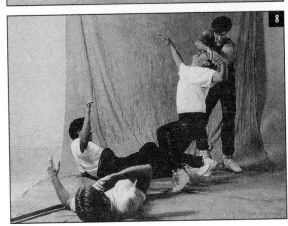

1   Burton is surrounded.

2   As one attacker begins to strike,

3   Burton rushes the farthest attacker. This puts him away from the first two attackers, and he gets to use the element of surprise on the third.

4   Burton grabs him by the arm and neck,

5   knees him, and prepares to throw,

6   the third attacker into the first two.

7   Burton finishes off the remaining attacker by palming his head,

8   and spinning him to make a takedown easier.

FINAL THOUGHTS

Some say that when you fight, you must hate your opponent. This is very low thinking and damages your attitude in life towards others and yourself. Rather than fight out of hate for your assailant, fight for the love of yourself and those who you love. If you are killed, your loved ones will be hurt emotionally, and your immediate family will be hurt financially as well. If you must fight, fight ferociously, but fight out of love.

At the highest level the JKD fighter should be a calm, nice, happy person who is easy to talk to and associate with. This is the state of being unless fighting or training with the fighting spirit.

Always strive to better yourself in every area of your life. As Pendekar Paul deThouars says, "Be yourself, but be the *BEST* of yourself!"

To contact Burton Richardson, or for more information on Jeet Kune Do Unlimited Membership, Seminars, Phase Testing, or Certification, call or write to the international headquarters:

Burton Richardson
Jeet Kune Do Unlimited
934 Hermosa Ave. #5
Hermosa Beach, CA 90254

310-318-6866 Telephone
310-318-8535 Fax

or visit the Jeet Kune Do Unlimited website at **www.jkdunlimited.com**